jewish

jewish

TRADITIONAL RECIPES FROM A RICH CULINARY HERITAGE

judy jackson

southwater

This edition is published by Southwater

Southwater is an imprint of Anness Publishing Ltd
Hermes House, 88–89 Blackfriars Road, London SE1 8HA
tel. 020 7401 2077; fax 020 7633 9499
www.southwaterbooks.com; info@anness.com

UK agent: The Manning Partnership Ltd, 6 The Old Dairy, Melcombe Road, Bath BA2 3LR; tel. 01225 478444; fax 01225 478440;
sales@manning-partnership.co.uk
UK distributor: Grantham Book Services Ltd, Isaac Newton Way, Alma Park Industrial Estate, Grantham, Lincs NG31 9SD; tel. 01476
541080; fax 01476 541061; orders@gbs.tbs-ltd.co.uk
North American agent/distributor: National Book Network, 4501 Forbes Boulevard, Suite 200, Lanham, MD 20706; tel. 301 459 3366;
fax 301 429 5746; www.nbnbooks.com
Australian agent/distributor: Pan Macmillan Australia, Level 18, St Martins Tower, 31 Market St, Sydney, NSW 2000; tel. 1300 135 113;
fax 1300 135 103; customer.service@macmillan.com.au
New Zealand agent/distributor: David Bateman Ltd, 30 Tarndale Grove, Off Bush Road, Albany, Auckland; tel. (09) 415 7664; fax (09)
415 8892

A CIP catalogue record for this book is available from the British Library.

Publisher Joanna Lorenz
Senior Cookery Editor Linda Fraser
Designer Ian Sandom
Illustrator Madeleine David
Photographer Amanda Heywood
Stylist Clare Louise Hunt
This edition is an edited version of the original work of Judy Jackson
Additional recipes pages 20, 21 and 46 Soheila Kimberley
page 44 Sarah Gates, page 56 Kit Chan

Cover:
Photographer Nicki Dowey; *Home Economist* Emma Patmore;
Design Wilson Harvey Marketing and Design

Previously published as part of the *Classic* cookery series

1 3 5 7 9 10 8 6 4 2

For all recipes, quantities are given in both metric and imperial measures, and, where appropriate, measures are also given in standard
cups and spoons. Follow one set, but not a mixture, because they are not interchangeable.

Picture on frontispiece: Whole Cooked Salmon with Stuffed Vegetables

CONTENTS

INTRODUCTION

For centuries, Jews have moved from country to country, taking their customs and cooking pots with them. The result is that Jewish cuisine is enormously varied. Observant Jews have always kept to rigid rules set down in the Old Testament about what they can and can't eat. So wherever they settled they found new foods and adapted them to complement the dishes they already knew. There are two distinct Jewish groups: one is Sephardi (broadly from the Mediterranean, the Middle and Far East), the other is Ashkenazi (from France, Germany, Russia and eastern Europe). Sephardi foods include ingredients more frequently found in Southern European countries – Spain, Italy or Greece – olive oil, vegetable or meat-stuffed peppers and aubergines, combined with exotic Middle Eastern fare, such as spicy rice from Iraq and Persia and sweet syrupy pastries from Turkey. Ashkenazi dishes feature heavier fare, ideal for the cold winters of eastern Europe: dumplings, soups, pulses, stews, hearty desserts and filling breads. This productive synthesis of culinary traditions is what makes Jewish cooking a unique and exciting experience.

Cooking the Jewish way is a rewarding, nourishing and enjoyable pastime. Eating is a social occasion, a time for family and friends to come together and share one of life's greatest pleasures. There are many causes for celebrations and festivals during the Jewish calendar where food assumes a central role – Passover, *Rosh Hashanah* (the Jewish New Year) or a barmitzvah – all are celebrated with eating and drinking.

Luckily, with the aid of modern technology such as mixers and blenders, the modern cook can now tackle time-consuming dishes with ease. So, whether you are are keen to explore the fascinating traditions of Jewish cooking for yourself or your family, or are cooking for Jewish friends, these recipes provide a valuable and informative introduction to cooking the Jewish way.

Opposite: clockwise from top left, a selection of classic Jewish breads and desserts: Coconut Pyramids, Challah, Peach Kuchen, Date Bread and Cinnamon Balls.

RITUALS AND TRADITIONS

Food is a vital part of the Jewish cultural and religious tradition. The end of week celebration is called the Shabbat, or the Sabbath. Each Friday and Saturday, the whole family comes together over long and delicious meals. Work is not allowed on Sabbaths or Festivals. Since cooking is considered work – however enjoyable – everything has to be prepared beforehand. So cooks have devised recipes that can be made before Friday evening or left to cook slowly overnight for lunch the next day. For both meals, the table is set with a fine white cloth

Clockwise from top right: noodles, barley, lockshen, matzo *and bulgur.*

and the best china and glass. There is always wine and plaited white loaves called *challah*. The classic Shabbat dish would have been a large stuffed fish, but in hard times inventive cooks adapted the dish to Gefilte Fish Balls, small balls of chopped fish now served at the beginning of a meal. The best-known Shabbat dish is called *cholent*, which is a large casserole full of meat, vegetables and a combination of beans, barley, chick-peas or potatoes. Designed for overnight cooking, it is a perfect all-in-one dish.

Another important festival is Passover. The *Seder*, or special meal, is eaten to symbolize the "passing over" of the Israelites when God ordered the death of first-born

Clockwise from top left: pitta bread, matzo crackers, round matzo crackers and bagels.

Egyptian sons, in biblical times. No leavened breads, cereals, biscuits or flour are eaten during this time. Unleavened bread is eaten instead, and nut cakes and dumplings are specially made. Other important festivals include *Rosh Hashanah* or New Year, when honey cakes are eaten in the hope that the coming year will be sweet.

The main rules observed in Jewish cuisine originate in the strict dietary laws or *kashrut* (from which the word "kosher" comes), laid down in the Old Testament. Forbidden ingredients include camel, hare, pig, shellfish, snails, monkfish, prawns, lobster, eels, octopus, birds of prey, any part of an "unclean" animal, or an animal that has not be killed humanely.

Meat dishes must not be mixed with dairy products either in a dish or immediately after each other – so creamy sauces with chicken, for instance, are forbidden, as is cheese after a meat dish, and coffee must be served black. However, dairy products can be mixed with fish dishes. If you are catering for observant Jewish friends, it is advisable to read the packaging on labels carefully, or opt for vegetarian dishes only. Many animal fats, gelatine and stocks contain pork-based products. Because of the strict separation between milk and meat, observant Jews keep separate utensils, so it is not uncommon to find two sets of crockery, saucepans and cutlery in the kitchen.

To balance the outlay in kitchen tools, Jewish dishes are often based on inexpensive ingredients, such as grains, pulses and vegetables. There are many one-pot dishes that use barley, noodles and lentils, which stretch a long way. Nuts are also widely used – ground and used instead of flour, added to stuffings, toasted or used to decorate fruit puddings or delicious salads. As with all cooking, the best-quality, freshest ingredients will bring the tastiest, most nutritious results.

A selection of fresh and dried fruits and nuts.

TOMATO AND RED PEPPER SOUP

A late summer soup using very ripe peppers and tomatoes. It won't be nearly as tasty if made with imported winter vegetables, which have a less distinctive flavour. It can be served cold.

INGREDIENTS
5 large tomatoes
30–60ml/2–4 tbsp olive oil
1 onion, chopped
450g/1lb thinly sliced red or orange peppers
30ml/2 tbsp tomato purée
a pinch of sugar
475ml/16fl oz/2 cups vegetable stock
60ml/4 tbsp soured cream (optional)
salt and ground black pepper
chopped fresh dill, to garnish

SERVES 4

1 Skin the tomatoes by plunging them into boiling water for 30 seconds. Chop the flesh and reserve any juice.

2 Heat half the oil in a saucepan and sauté the onion over moderate heat until soft.

3 Add the peppers and the remaining oil and continue cooking, without browning the vegetables, until they start to soften.

COOK'S TIP
To make a light vegetable stock, simply boil some carrots, onion, leek or root vegetables in a large pan of water. Simmer for about 30 minutes and then strain.

4 Stir in the chopped tomatoes, tomato purée, the seasoning, sugar and a few tablespoons of stock and simmer until the vegetables are tender.

5 Stir the rest of the stock and blend until smooth. Strain to remove the skins, and season with salt and pepper.

6 Pour into bowls, swirl in the cream, if using, and garnish with dill.

JERUSALEM ARTICHOKE SOUP

An ideal soup for cold weather as it is thick, warming and nourishing. It is traditionally eaten at Passover, accompanied by matzo crackers.

INGREDIENTS
30–60ml/2–4 tbsp butter
115g/4oz/2 cups sliced mushrooms
2 onions, chopped
450g/1lb Jerusalem artichokes, peeled and sliced
300ml/½ pint/1¼ cups vegetable stock
300ml/½ pint/1¼ cups milk
salt and ground black pepper

SERVES 4

1 Melt the butter in a saucepan and sauté the mushrooms for about 1 minute. Put them on a plate and place in a very low oven to keep warm.

2 Sauté the onions and artichokes in the saucepan, adding a little more butter if necessary. Keep on stirring the vegetables without allowing them to brown.

COOK'S TIP
Any type of mushrooms can be used for this soup, or a mixture if desired. Dark varieties such as chestnut mushrooms will give the soup a deep colour.

3 Add the vegetable stock to the pan and bring to the boil. Simmer until the artichokes are soft, then season to taste.

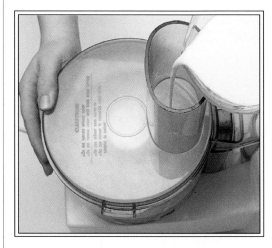

4 Purée the soup with a hand blender or food processor, adding the milk slowly until smooth. Reheat the soup, return the mushrooms to the pan and serve.

CHICKEN SOUP WITH LOCKSHEN

Known as the "Jewish penicillin", chicken soup is simple to make, if you follow two rules: make it the day before, and use a boiling fowl, which has much more flavour than a roasting bird.

INGREDIENTS
3kg/6¹/₂lb boiling chicken, including the
giblets, but not the liver
1 litre/1³/₄ pints/4 cups cold water
2 onions, halved
2 carrots
5 celery sticks
a handful (about 115g/4oz) fine
vermicelli (lockshen)
salt and ground black pepper

SERVES 6 – 8

1 Put the washed chicken into a very large pan with the giblets. Add the water and bring to the boil over high heat. Skim off the white froth that comes to the top, and then add the halved onions, carrots and sticks of celery. Season with ground black pepper only.

2 When the liquid comes to the boil again, turn the heat to low, cover and simmer the chicken and the stock for at least 2 hours. Keep an eye on the water level and add a little more so that the chicken is always covered.

3 When the chicken is tender, remove from the pan and take the meat off the bones, reserving it for another use. Put the bones back in the soup and continue cooking for a further 1 hour. There should be at least 1 litre/1¾ pints/4 cups of soup.

4 Strain the soup into a large bowl and chill the liquid part overnight in the refrigerator. When it is quite cold, it may form a jelly with a pale layer of fat settled on the top. Remove the fat with a spoon and discard.

5 When you are ready to serve the soup, transfer the cold mixture into a saucepan and bring to the boil again. Season with salt and freshly ground black pepper to taste, and add the vermicelli (*lockshen*). Boil for a further 8–10 minutes. Serve in large bowls.

CHICKEN SOUP WITH MATZO KLEIS BALLS

During Passover when no leavened bread or pasta is eaten, chicken soup is served with dumplings. There are many kinds of dumplings or *knaidlach*, all of Ashkenazi (eastern European) origin. The secret of making them light is to keep the mixture soft, and to chill the dumplings before cooking.

INGREDIENTS

2 matzot (sheets of unleavened bread)
1 onion, chopped
30ml/2 tbsp oil
a handful of parsley
2 eggs
pinch of ground ginger
15ml/1 tbsp medium-ground matzo meal
1 quantity chicken soup (see recipe for Chicken Soup with Lockshen)
salt and ground black pepper

SERVES 12

1 Soak the matzot in cold water for about 5 minutes. Drain and squeeze them in your hands until dry.

2 Fry the onion in the oil until golden. Chop the parsley, reserving a few sprigs to garnish. Whisk the eggs slightly.

3 Mix together the soaked matzot, fried onion, chopped parsley and whisked egg in a large bowl. Season with salt, freshly ground black pepper and ginger to taste, and add the matzo meal. Chill for at least 1 hour in the refrigerator, until completely cold and firm.

4 Roll the mixture into small balls using the palm of your hand. Carefully drop the balls, one at a time, into the fast-boiling soup and cook for about 20 minutes. Serve, garnished with the parsley.

15

BARLEY SOUP

Eastern Europe has bitter winters so traditional soups often contained a mixture of filling ingredients such as beans, lentils and barley.

INGREDIENTS
900g/2lb meaty bones (lamb, beef or veal)
900ml/1½ pints/3¾ cups water
3 carrots
4 celery sticks
1 onion
30ml/2 tbsp oil
30ml/2 tbsp barley
salt and ground black pepper

SERVES 4

1 Preheat the oven to 200°C/400°F/Gas 6. To prepare the meat stock, brown the lamb, beef or veal bones in a roasting tin in the oven for about 30 minutes. Remove the bones and put them in a large saucepan, cover with water and bring to the boil.

2 With a metal spoon skim off the froth on the surface and cover the pan. Simmer for at least 2 hours. Chop the carrots, celery and onion finely. Heat the oil in a saucepan and sauté the vegetables in the oil for about 1 minute. Strain the stock into the pan.

3 Add the barley to the pan of vegetables and continue cooking for about 1 hour, until the barley is soft. Season the soup with plenty of salt and pepper, transfer to serving bowls and serve hot.

COOK'S TIP
All soups taste better with home-made stock. The long, slow simmering can be done in advance and stocks freeze well. A quick (and more salty) version can be made using water and a stock cube, but it won't have the same flavour.

CHOPPED LIVER WITH EGG AND ONION

Traditionally, chicken fat was used in this recipe and the mixture chopped by hand. This modern version uses chicken stock and a blender.

INGREDIENTS
FOR THE LIVER PÂTÉ
225g/8oz/1¼ cups chicken livers
45ml/3 tbsp oil
1 onion, chopped
45ml/3 tbsp chicken stock

FOR THE EGG AND ONION
2–3 eggs, hard-boiled and shelled
2–3 spring onions, chopped
30ml/2 tbsp chicken stock
salt and ground black pepper
red spring onion strips, to garnish
bread, black olives and gherkins, to serve

SERVES 4

1 Preheat the grill. Place the chicken livers on an oiled wire rack in a grill pan and cook under the grill for about 2–3 minutes on each side.

2 Heat the oil in a frying pan and sauté the onion until golden. Add the livers and cook briefly, breaking them up with a fork so that they are no longer pink inside. Season.

3 Add the chicken stock, turn down the heat and continue cooking the liver and onions for a few minutes. Spoon them into a blender or food processor and process into a smooth paste. Remove the chopped liver.

4 To make the egg and onion mixture, put the eggs with the spring onion in the bowl of the blender or food processor. There's no need to wash it first; it does no harm to flavour the eggs with a little bit of chopped liver. Add the stock, season and blend until smooth.

5 Serve the chopped liver in a small mound with some of the egg and onion on the side. Garnish with red spring onion strips and serve with fresh bread, black olives and gherkins.

HUMMUS

Traditionally served with falafel, this chick-pea and sesame seed dip is also good with crackers or raw vegetables. The tahina, or sesame seed paste, is available from Jewish and Arabic delicatessens. It's worth making a large quantity as hummus freezes well.

INGREDIENTS
225g/8oz/1¼ cups chick-peas, soaked overnight
115g/4oz/½ cup tahina paste
2 garlic cloves, crushed
juice of 1–2 lemons
30ml/2 tbsp olive oil
salt and ground black pepper
cayenne pepper, chopped parsley and black olives, to garnish

SERVES 4

1 Drain the chick-peas and cook in fresh boiling water for 10 minutes. Reduce the heat and simmer for about an hour or until soft. Drain the chick-peas, reserving the cooking liquid.

2 Put the chick-peas into a food processor, add the tahina paste, garlic and a little lemon juice. Process until smooth. Season with salt and ground black pepper, and add enough cooking liquid to process until creamy. Add more lemon juice or liquid as the hummus stiffens after resting.

3 Spoon the hummus on to a plate, swirl with a knife and drizzle with olive oil. Sprinkle with cayenne pepper, chopped parsley and the black olives, to garnish.

FALAFEL

A typical street food in Israel, hot, crispy falafel are served in warm pitta bread. They make an excellent starter or buffet dish.

INGREDIENTS
450g/1lb/2½ cups dried
white beans or chick-peas
2 red onions, chopped
2 large garlic cloves, crushed
45ml/3 tbsp fresh parsley,
finely chopped
5ml/1 tsp ground coriander
5ml/1 tsp ground cumin
7.5ml/1½ tsp baking powder
oil, for deep frying
salt and ground black pepper
quartered tomatoes and torn basil
leaves, to serve

SERVES 6

1 Soak the beans or chick-peas in water overnight. Drain and discard the water.

2 Remove the skins from the beans and process them in a blender or food processor. Add the chopped onions, garlic, parsley, coriander, cumin, baking powder and seasoning and blend again to make a smooth paste. Allow the mixture to stand at room temperature for at least 30 minutes.

3 Take walnut-sized pieces of mixture and, using the palm of your hand, roll into small balls.

4 Heat the oil until it is very hot and then fry the balls in batches until golden. Drain on kitchen paper and serve with quartered tomatoes and torn basil leaves.

> #### COOK'S TIP
> Canned chick-peas can be used instead of white beans or dried chick-peas. Drain and rinse under cold water before processing.

WHOLE COOKED SALMON

The availability of farmed salmon has made this fish more affordable and less of a treat than it used to be. As with all fish, the delicious taste depends on freshness and not overcooking.

INGREDIENTS

2.25–3kg/5–6½ lb fresh whole salmon
30ml/2 tbsp oil
1 lemon
salt and ground black pepper
lemon wedges, cucumber and fresh dill
sprigs, to garnish
green salad and mayonnaise, to serve

SERVES 10

1 Preheat the oven to 200ºC/400ºF/Gas 6. Wash the salmon and dry it well, inside and out. Pour half the oil on to a large piece of foil and place the fish in the centre.

2 Put several slices of lemon inside the salmon and arrange some more on the top. Season well and sprinkle the remaining oil over the fish.

3 Wrap up the foil to make a loose parcel. Put the parcel on another sheet of foil or a baking sheet and cook in the oven for approximately 10 minutes. Turn off the oven; don't open the door and leave for 2–3 hours. The salmon will cook in the warmth of the oven, remaining moist and tender.

> #### COOK'S TIP
> Other fish, such as bream, cod and halibut, can be cooked in a similar way: wrapped in foil and baked in a hot oven with the heat turned off.

4 To serve the same day, remove the foil and peel off the skin. If you are keeping it for the following day, leave the skin on and chill the fish overnight in the refrigerator. Arrange the fish on a large platter and garnish with lemon wedges, cucumber cut into thin ribbons and sprigs of dill. Traditionally, this dish is served with green salad and mayonnaise.

GEFILTE FISH

There are two ways of cooking this popular dish, either by poaching or frying. It is eaten at the Sabbath meal, and often made as a starter to accompany *cholent*, a rich meat stew. This dish was created in hard times, as a cheap alternative to an expensive whole fish. A variety of fish can be used.

INGREDIENTS
900g/2lb mixed filleted fish, such as carp, bream, haddock and cod
1 large onion
2 eggs
5–10ml/1–2 tsp sugar
50g/2oz/10 tbsp medium-ground matzo meal
oil, for frying
salt and ground black pepper
flat leaf parsley, to garnish
bottled beetroot and horseradish sauce, to serve

MAKES 24 SMALL BALLS

1 Cut the fish and the onion into small pieces and mix together in a food processor. Add the eggs, sugar, salt and pepper and continue to blend until smooth.

2 Stir in a few spoonfuls of matzo meal and form into 2.5cm/1in balls. The mixture will seem quite soft.

3 Roll the balls in the remaining matzo meal and chill them in the refrigerator until you are ready to fry them. When ready, heat a large pan of oil until it reaches a temperature of 190ºC/375ºF. Fry the balls for about 4–5 minutes until they are crisp and golden brown.

4 Lift them out with a slotted spoon and drain thoroughly. Cool.

5 Garnish with flat leaf parsley and serve cold, with beetroot and horseradish sauce, if liked.

CUCUMBER AND FISH SALAD

A cool dish for summer – ideal served on individual plates for lunch or on a large platter as part of a buffet. Instead of cod you can use haddock fillet or, for a more special occasion, sea bass.

INGREDIENTS
2 large cucumbers
500g/1¼ lb cod fillet, skinned
1 spring onion, chopped
a small bunch of fresh dill
75ml/5 tbsp milk
60ml/4 tbsp mayonnaise
30ml/2 tbsp crème fraîche
175g/6oz/¾ cup cooked broad beans
or peas (optional)
salt
cucumber ribbons, to garnish
4–8 black or green olives, to serve

SERVES 4 – 8

1 Skin one of the cucumbers and cut the flesh into dice. Using a vegetable peeler, remove about six long thin strips from the other cucumber and then dice as well. Sprinkle each piece with salt and leave to drain on absorbent kitchen paper for approximately 10 minutes.

2 Put the fish in a pan with the spring onion, a sprig of dill and the milk. Season well and poach for a few minutes until the fish begins to flake. Test with a fork, then lift out with a slotted spoon and leave to cool.

3 Wash and drain the salted cucumber cubes and dry thoroughly. Mix the mayonnaise with the crème fraîche. Stir in the cucumber, broad beans or peas, if using, and finally fold in the fish.

4 Spoon the mixture on to plates, and garnish with cucumber ribbons. Serve with black and green olives, if liked.

COOK'S TIP
You can substitute natural, set yogurt for mayonnaise as a lighter option, if liked.

HALIBUT IN LEMON SAUCE

tart lemony sauce perfectly complements chunky halibut steak. This dish can be eaten hot or cold.

INGREDIENTS
1 small onion
1 large carrot
2.5ml/¹/₂ tsp sugar
4 halibut steaks
2 lemons
3 egg yolks
salt and ground black pepper
asparagus and boiled potatoes, to serve

SERVES 4

1 Slice the onion and carrot and bring to the boil in a deep saucepan. Add the sugar and season with salt and pepper, then simmer for 15 minutes. Remove the vegetable pieces with a slotted spoon and put aside.

2 Lower the halibut steaks into the pan containing the vegetable cooking liquid and cook over low heat for 8–10 minutes. To check when the halibut steaks are cooked, insert a knife near the bone; if the fish looks opaque it is cooked. Lift the steaks out of the pan and arrange on a shallow dish.

3 Bring the cooking liquid to the boil again and reduce it over high heat for a few minutes. This will form the base of the lemon sauce.

COOK'S TIP
This lemon sauce is extremely versatile and can be used to accompany any white fish, such as cod or hake.

4 Cut a few slices from the top of each lemon and set aside for garnishing. Squeeze the juice from the lemons, whisk the egg yolks lightly in a bowl and stir in the lemon juice.

5 Strain the cooking liquid on to the egg and lemon mixture and pour it back into the pan. Stir the sauce over a low heat, taking care not to let it boil. When it thickens, pour over the fish. Serve the fish with asparagus and boiled potatoes.

FRIED FISH

This dish is nearly always served cold. If you have never tried it, you are missing a real speciality. A tray of different fish is customary, but you can use one variety if you prefer. The usual accompaniment is potato salad.

INGREDIENTS
2 Dover sole, about 225g/8oz each
2 large plaice, about 450g/1lb each
1 thick cod fillet, about 450g/1lb, skinned
1.5 litres/2½ pints/6¼ cups oil
45ml/3 tbsp flour
40–50g/1½–2oz/8–10 tbsp medium-ground matzo meal
4 eggs
salt and ground black pepper
lemon wedges, to garnish
potato salad and pickled cucumber, to serve

SERVES 8

1 Wash and dry the fish thoroughly. Leave the Dover sole whole, but cut the plaice across the main bone in the centre into three sections. Cut the cod fillet into two or three equal pieces.

2 Begin to heat the oil in a large deep pan. It will take 4–6 minutes for 2.5cm/1in of oil to reach a hot enough temperature (approximately 190ºC/375ºF). If you don't have a thermometer, then carefully drop a cube of bread into the oil; if it browns in 30 seconds then your oil is ready.

3 Put the flour and the matzo meal on large, separate plates or shallow dishes. Break the eggs into a glass bowl, season and whisk lightly. Season the flour and the matzo meal.

4 Dip each piece of fish first into the flour and then into the beaten egg. Lift out immediately and dip it into the matzo meal. Cover each piece thoroughly.

5 Lower the fish into the hot oil. Don't put in too many pieces as this reduces the temperature of the oil. Fry each piece for about 6 minutes. Turn the fish over and when it is crisp and brown, lift it out with a slotted spoon. Drain over the oil and cool on kitchen paper. Serve with potato salad and pickled cucumbers, garnished with lemon.

STUFFED COURGETTES

his recipe can be adapted to suit a range of other vegetables; peppers, onions or tomatoes.

INGREDIENTS
4 courgettes
30–60ml/2–4 tbsp olive oil
225g/8oz/1 cup basmati rice
2 dried peaches or apricots
1.5ml/¹/₄ tsp tomato purée
pinch of ground cinnamon
1.5ml/¹/₄ tsp paprika
a small bunch of flat leaf parsley
salt and ground black pepper

SERVES 6 – 8

1 Preheat the oven to 190ºC/375ºF/Gas 5. Cut off the ends of the courgettes and remove the centres with a corer.

2 Heat half the oil in a roasting tin for about 5 minutes. Add the courgettes and roast for about 20 minutes. Drizzle the remaining oil over the top.

3 Meanwhile cook the rice. Rinse the rice thoroughly with hot water. Bring a large saucepan of water to the boil, add the rice and boil for about 8 minutes or until tender, but not mushy. Drain and rinse the rice again to remove any starch.

4 Snip the dried peach or apricot into slivers with kitchen scissors, and stir into the rice with the tomato purée, spices and seasoning. Chop some of the parsley and mix about 45ml/3 tbsp into the rice. Pour a little oil used to roast the courgettes into the rice.

5 Cool the courgettes slightly and stuff with the rice. Arrange on a serving dish. Garnish with parsley. Serve hot or cold.

AUBERGINES WITH CHEESE

C heese is never served with meat, or as a separate course after meat. However, it often features as part of a fish or vegetarian buffet.

INGREDIENTS
2 large aubergines
450g/1lb tomatoes
1 onion
75–105ml/5–7 tbsp olive oil
175g/6oz kosher Dutch or Cheddar
cheese, thinly sliced
salt and ground black pepper
green salad, to serve

SERVES 4

1 Cut the aubergines crossways into 1cm/½in slices. Sprinkle with salt and leave to drain on kitchen paper for 30 minutes. Rinse well and dry. Skin and slice the tomatoes.

2 Chop the onion finely and sauté it in a few tablespoons of olive oil until golden. Set aside on a plate. Heat the remaining oil and fry the aubergine slices on both sides until brown. Season the vegetables lightly.

3 Preheat the oven to 190°C/375°F/Gas 5. Put a layer of aubergine slices into an oiled casserole. Sprinkle over some of the onion and then add some tomato slices. Cover with slices of cheese and continue making layers until all the ingredients are used up, finishing with a layer of cheese.

4 Bake for 30–40 minutes until the cheese is bubbling and brown. Serve with a green salad.

MATZO PANCAKES

Passover pancakes are made with matzo meal instead of flour. Flour is never used at Passover, in memory of the flight from Egypt, when the Jews, fleeing from the tyrannical Pharaoh, left with such haste that they did not have time to let their bread rise.

INGREDIENTS
FOR THE PANCAKES
1 egg white
1 whole egg
120ml/4fl oz/¹⁄₂ cup water
pinch salt
40g/1¹⁄₂oz/8 tbsp fine-ground matzo meal
30–45ml/2–3 tbsp oil

FOR THE SAVOURY TOPPING
225g/8oz fresh spinach
50g/2oz/¹⁄₂ cup Cheddar cheese, grated
salt and ground black pepper

MAKES 10 PANCAKES

1 For the topping: wash the spinach very well, drain and cook in a pan with no extra water for 1 minute. Put it in a sieve, press out the moisture with a spoon. Remove the spinach from the sieve, chop it, season and stir in half the cheese.

2 For the pancakes, whisk the egg white and the whole egg until thick and then gradually add the water and salt. Sprinkle in the matzo meal and beat until smooth.

> ### COOK'S TIP
> Matzo pancakes can also be served as a dessert, sprinkled with a liberal amount of sugar and a pinch of ground cinnamon.

3 Heat a little of the oil in a small frying pan and when it is hot, drop some of the mixture in large spoonfuls into the oil. Almost immediately turn them over and press the pancakes down slightly. Cook for another minute on the other side.

4 Repeat until the mixture is used up. While you are cooking the pancakes, heat the grill. Arrange the pancakes in the grill pan. Cover each one with a little of the spinach mixture and top with the remaining cheese. Grill for 1–2 minutes to melt the cheese and serve immediately.

ROASTED LAMB WITH COURGETTES

Racks of tender lamb chops, roasted pink on the inside, are a favourite choice for wedding dinners.

INGREDIENTS
2 small racks lamb, each with 6 chops
60ml/4 tbsp olive oil
juice of 1 pomegranate
15ml/1 tbsp French mustard
4 mint leaves
4 courgettes, quartered lengthways
120ml/4fl oz/½ cup light vegetable or
chicken stock
30ml/2 tbsp toasted pine nuts
salt and ground black pepper
1 sprig fresh mint, to garnish

SERVES 4

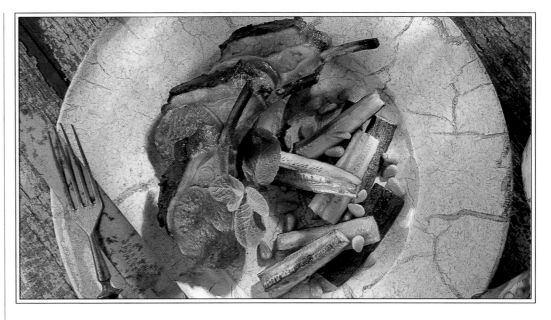

1 Arrange the racks of lamb in a glass or ceramic dish. In a glass jug, mix together 15ml/1 tbsp olive oil, the pomegranate juice, mustard, salt and pepper. Add the mint leaves and pour half of this marinade over the lamb. Chill for a couple of hours.

2 Preheat the oven to 230°C/450°F/Gas 8. Pour the remaining oil into a dish and put in the oven to heat. Add the courgettes to the hot oil, turning them over to coat both sides.

3 Put the lamb in a roasting tin, fat side up. Add the courgettes. Roast the lamb and courgettes for 20 minutes.

4 Transfer the racks of lamb to a serving dish and let rest for 5 minutes, covered with a sheet of foil. Remove the courgettes. Pour the remaining marinade and stock into the roasting tin. Stir over the heat to deglaze the meat juices and pour into a sauce boat.

COOK'S TIP
To make pomegranate juice, halve the fruit and squeeze like a lemon.

5 Slice each rack of lamb into chops and arrange them on plates. Sprinkle the pine nuts over the courgettes. Serve the sauce separately and garnish the lamb with a sprig of mint.

SLOW-COOKED LAMB WITH BARLEY

perfect Sabbath dish, which can be left cooking for many hours. It really is worth the wait!

INGREDIENTS

15–30ml/1–2 tbsp oil
900g/2lb shoulder of lamb, cubed
2 large onions
6 carrots or potatoes
115g/4oz/²⁄₃ cup barley
750ml–1.2 litres/1¹⁄₄–2 pints/3–5 cups
boiling stock or 1 kosher beef stock cube
dissolved in water
chopped thyme, to garnish
salt and ground black pepper

SERVES 4 – 6

COOK'S TIP
A slow-cooker is ideal for long, gentle cooking as it does not dry up the gravy. If you are using a conventional oven for slow cooking, at 110°C/225°F/Gas ¼, the liquid tends to evaporate, so it's a good idea to add a little more liquid than specified.

1 Heat half the oil in a non-stick frying pan and sauté the cubes of lamb until brown all over. Transfer the meat to a large plate.

2 Cut the onions and carrots into small pieces (or thinly slice the potatoes, if using), and sauté these in the remaining oil. Add the barley and seasoning, pour in half the stock and bring the liquid to the boil. Cook for about 5 minutes.

3 Pour the vegetables and barley into the base of a slow-cooker, cover with the lamb cubes and add enough stock to make a gravy. (See Cook's Tip.) Cover and cook for 6–9 hours or more. Check for seasoning, stir well and serve garnished with thyme.

LAMB WITH LENTILS AND APRICOTS

A warming one-pot meal ideal for a cold winter's evening, with a delicate sweetness provided by the dried apricots.

INGREDIENTS

2 large onions
2 large carrots
30–60ml/2–4 tbsp oil
900g/2lb lean lamb
2.5ml/1/2 tsp ground cinnamon or
2.5cm/1in cinnamon stick
1.5ml/1/4 tsp ground turmeric
1.5ml/1/4 tsp chilli powder
225g/8oz/1 cup green lentils
1 litre/1 3/4 pints/4 cups water
12 ready-to-eat dried apricots
salt and ground black pepper
chopped fresh parsley, to garnish

SERVES 4 – 6

1 Preheat the oven to 180ºC/350ºF/Gas 4. Cut the onions and carrots into large chunks. Heat half the oil in a flameproof casserole and sauté the vegetables until the onion starts to brown. Put the vegetables on a plate and set aside.

2 Cut the lamb into 2.5cm/1in cubes and sauté over medium heat, adding more oil if necessary to brown them all over. Add the ground cinnamon or cinnamon stick and sprinkle the rest of the spices over the lamb.

3 Rinse the lentils and add to the casserole with the vegetables. Stir in 750ml/1 1/4 pints/3 cups boiling water, season and bring to boil. Cover and transfer to the oven.

4 Cook for 1 hour. Check frequently to ensure that the lentils haven't absorbed all the liquid, adding the remaining water if necessary. Cook for a further hour until the lentils are soft.

5 Add the apricots and press them down until covered by the gravy. Turn off the oven and leave the apricots to swell for about 20 minutes. Season with salt and ground black pepper to taste, and stir in a little more water if it seems too dry. Garnish with chopped parsley.

STEAK SALAD

I n most countries, kosher beef comes from the forequarter, so it lacks the tenderness of fillet and rump. Rare-cooked steak with vegetables makes a well-flavoured main course salad.

INGREDIENTS
500g/1¼lb new potatoes
115g/4oz young carrots
1 sprig mint
225g/8oz French beans
450g/1lb rare-grilled steak or cooked roast beef
150ml/¼ pint/⅔ cup mayonnaise
salt and ground black pepper
1 sliced yellow pepper, lettuce leaves and 4 black olives, to garnish

SERVES 4

1 Wash the potatoes and carrots and leave whole. Cook them separately in boiling salted water with a few mint leaves for added flavour. When the vegetables are tender, pour them into a colander and leave to drain thoroughly. Cook the French beans for a few minutes in boiling salted water or until they are just tender. Drain, and leave the beans to cool.

2 Cut the rare-grilled steak or cooked roast beef into small dice. Mix the vegetables with mayonnaise and fold in the meat. Season to taste.

3 Pile the steak salad high into the centre of a large dish and garnish with sliced yellow pepper, crisp lettuce leaves and the black olives.

BEEF CHOLENT WITH BEANS AND HAMIN EGGS

There are many different versions of this classic, slow-cooked casserole. This one has the addition of whole eggs, which are cooked in their shells.

INGREDIENTS
225g/8oz/1¼ cups haricot or butter beans
6–8 small eggs
10 small onions
2 carrots
30–60ml/2–4 tbsp oil
1.5kg/3–3½lb stewing steak, cubed
5ml/1 tsp paprika
5ml/1 tsp tomato purée
600ml/1 pint/2½ cups boiling water or beef stock
salt and ground black pepper

SERVES 6 – 8

COOK'S TIP
For overnight cooking, a slow-cooker is the best method since the liquid does not evaporate. If you are using a conventional oven, cook the *cholent* overnight at 110°C/225°F/Gas ¼, but be sure to add enough water or stock to almost fill the pot.

1 Soak the beans in cold water overnight. Drain and bring to the boil in fresh water. Cook rapidly for 10 minutes, skimming off the white froth and any bean skins that come to the surface. Drain and reserve the cooking liquid for another use.

2 Boil the eggs in salted water for about 10 minutes, until hard. Leave the eggs in their shells and set aside.

3 Preheat a slow-cooker to auto. Halve the onions and dice the carrots. Heat half the oil in a pan and sauté the onions until brown. Then transfer to the slow-cooker with the carrots and beans. Brown the beef in the remaining oil and place on top of the vegetables. Arrange the eggs in between the pieces of meat.

4 Stir the paprika, tomato purée and seasoning into the remaining oil and cook for 1 minute. Add the boiling water or stock to deglaze the pan and pour over the meat and eggs.

5 Cover the pot and leave to cook for between 8–20 hours. Remove the eggs with a slotted spoon, shell them and return them to the casserole before serving.

COLD SLICED ROAST CHICKEN

Cooking chestnut stuffing under the skin of the bird keeps the breast meat succulent and creates a striped effect when carved.

INGREDIENTS
2 onions
30–45ml/2–3 tbsp oil
65g/2¹/₂oz/1¹/₄ cups fresh breadcrumbs
200g/7oz/³/₄ cup unsweetened chestnut purée
2.25kg/5¹/₄ lb fresh, free-range chicken
salt and ground black pepper
flat leaf parsley, to garnish
potatoes, crushed pistachio nuts and lettuce leaves, to serve

SERVES 6 – 8

1 Finely chop one onion. Heat half of the oil in a small pan and sauté half of the onion until golden. Stir in 120ml/4fl oz/¹/₂ cup boiling water, take the pan off the heat and leave to stand for 5 minutes to absorb some of the liquid.

2 Mix together the breadcrumbs, the remaining chopped onion and chestnut purée with the sautéd onion and any liquid in the pan. Season well. Leave to cool.

3 Preheat the over to 220ºC/425ºF/Gas 7. Wipe the chicken well with kitchen paper, inside and out, and carefully slide your hand under the skin on the breast to ease it away from the meat. Press the stuffing underneath the skin all over the breast.

4 Brush a roasting tin with the remaining oil and put in the chicken, breast side down, with the remaining onion, halved. Roast for 1 hour, basting occasionally and pouring away any excess fat.

5 Turn the chicken over so that the breast is uppermost and continue to roast for a further 15 minutes.

6 When cooked, leave the chicken to cool before cutting downwards into slices. Garnish with flat leaf parsley and serve with potatoes sprinkled with crushed pistachio nuts and lettuce leaves.

CHICKEN PIE WITH MUSHROOMS

This delicious pie uses chicken stock rather than the more familiar milk and butter.

INGREDIENTS
FOR THE PASTRY
150g/5oz kosher margarine, chilled
225g/8oz/2 cups plain flour
1 egg yolk
60ml/4 tbsp cold water

FOR THE FILLING
900g/2lb cooked roast or boiled chicken
45ml/3 tbsp olive oil
275g/10oz mixed dark mushrooms
(flat, oyster or chestnut)
25ml/1½ tbsp flour
300ml/½ pint/1¼ cups chicken stock
15ml/1 tbsp kosher soy sauce
1 egg white
salt and ground black pepper

SERVES 4 – 6

1 For the pastry, cut the margarine into small pieces and rub it into the flour until it is like breadcrumbs. Mix the egg yolk with the cold water and stir it into the flour mixture. Form the dough into a ball, cover and chill for about 30 minutes. Preheat the oven to 220°C/425°F/Gas 7.

2 For the filling, cut the chicken into pieces and put them in a greased, oven-proof pie dish with 1.75 litres/3 pints/7½ cups capacity.

3 Heat half the oil in a frying pan. Slice the mushrooms into thick pieces and sauté them over high heat for 3 minutes. Add the rest of the oil and slowly stir in the flour. Season with salt and pepper and slowly add the stock, stirring constantly to make a thick sauce. Stir in the soy sauce, and pour the mushroom sauce over the chicken.

4 Roll out the pastry and cut one piece slightly larger than the size of the pie dish. Also cut some long strips about 2cm/¾in wide. Place these round the rim of the dish, then lift the pastry on to the top, pressing it down on top of the strips. Knock up the edges with a knife. Slash the top of the pie in a chequerboard fashion.

5 Lightly whisk the egg white and brush it over the pie. Bake in the oven for about 30–35 minutes.

APPLE-STUFFED DUCK

S tuffing the duck breasts with whole apples keeps the meat moist and provides an attractive mix of colours when served cold.

INGREDIENTS
40g/1½ oz raisins or sultanas
30ml/2 tbsp kosher brandy
3 large onions
30ml/2 tbsp oil
175g/6oz fresh breadcrumbs
2 small apples, preferably Cox
2 large duck breasts, including the skin
salt and ground black pepper
mixed leaf salad, to serve

SERVES 4

1 Soak the dried fruit in the brandy. Preheat the oven to 220°C/425°F/Gas 7.

2 Chop one onion finely and sauté it in the oil until golden. Season with salt and pepper and add 50–120ml/2–4fl oz/¼–½ cup water. Bring to the boil and then add breadcrumbs until the stuffing is moist but not sloppy.

3 Core and peel the apples. Drain the raisins and press them into the centre of the apples. Flatten the duck breasts and spread out, skin side down.

4 Divide the stuffing between the breasts and spread over the meat. Place an apple at one end of each breast and carefully roll up to enclose the apples and stuffing. Secure with a length of cotton or fine string. Quarter the remaining onions. Prick the duck skin in several places to release the fat.

5 Arrange the duck breasts on a rack in a roasting tin with the onions underneath. Roast for about 35 minutes. Pour off the fat and roast at 160°C/325°F/Gas 3 for a further 30–40 minutes.

6 To serve cool, leave to get quite cold at room temperature and then chill in the refrigerator. Cut each breast into 5 or 6 thin slices. Arrange on a platter and bring to room temperature before serving. Serve with a mixed leaf salad.

TURKEY BREASTS WITH WINE AND GRAPES

P oultry and other meats are never cooked with cream or milk. This dish relies on a good stock and wine to provide the velvety sauce and a deliciously moist texture to the meat.

INGREDIENTS
450g/1lb turkey breast, thinly sliced
45ml/3 tbsp flour
45–90ml/3–6 tbsp oil
120ml/4fl oz/$^1\!/_2$ cup kosher white
wine or sherry
120ml/4fl oz/$^1\!/_2$ cup chicken stock
150g/5oz white grapes
salt and ground black pepper
flat leaf parsley, to garnish

SERVES 3

1 Put the turkey slices in between sheets of greaseproof paper and flatten with a rolling pin. Season the flour and coat both sides of each slice.

2 Heat the oil in a large frying pan and sauté the turkey slices for about 3 minutes on each side. Pour in the wine or sherry and boil rapidly to reduce it slightly.

3 Remove the turkey from the pan, set aside in a warm place. Stir in the chicken stock, lower the heat and cook for another few minutes. Halve and seed the grapes and stir into the sauce.

4 Pour the sauce over the turkey. Garnish with the flat leaf parsley and serve.

COOK'S TIP
For a dark sauce you could add chestnut mushrooms. Sauté them in oil before you cook the turkey in Step 2 and add to the stock in Step 3.

ROASTED PEPPER SALAD

This colourful salad can be served as either a starter or an attractive, colourful side dish to accompany cold meat or fish dishes.

INGREDIENTS
2 red peppers, halved and seeded
2 yellow peppers, halved and seeded
90–120ml/6–8 tbsp olive oil
1 onion, thinly sliced
2 garlic cloves, crushed
30ml/2 tbsp fresh lemon juice
salt and ground black pepper
chopped fresh parsley, to serve

SERVES 4

1 Preheat the oven to 190⁰C/375⁰F/Gas 5. Coat the peppers in the oil and arrange in a roasting tin. Roast for 5–10 minutes until the skin has blistered and blackened. Pop the peppers into a plastic bag, seal and leave for 5 minutes.

2 Meanwhile, heat 30ml/2 tbsp of the oil in a frying pan and add the onion. Fry for about 5–6 minutes, until softened. Remove from the heat and reserve.

COOK'S TIP
Other vegetables such as tomatoes and courgettes can be prepared in this way. When roasting courgettes, do not remove the skin in Step 3 and roast for 15-20 minutes.

3 Take the peppers out of the plastic bag and peel off the skins. Discard the skins and slice each pepper half into thin strips, about 2.5cm/1in wide.

4 Place the peppers, onions and any oil from the pan into a bowl. Add the crushed garlic and pour on the remaining olive oil, add the lemon juice and season. Mix well and garnish with parsley.

TABBOULEH

A salad that actually improves if it is made the day before. The bulgur, or cracked wheat, is uncooked and absorbs the moisture and flavour of the vegetables and dressing.

INGREDIENTS
175g/6oz/1 cup fine bulgur wheat
juice of 1 lemon
45ml/3 tbsp olive oil
40g/1¹/₂oz fresh parsley, finely chopped
45ml/3 tbsp fresh mint, chopped
4–5 spring onions, chopped
1 green pepper, seeded and sliced
salt and freshly ground black pepper
2 large tomatoes, diced, and 6 black
olives, to garnish

SERVES 4

1 Cover the bulgur wheat with cold water and leave to soak in a large bowl for 30 minutes or more.

2 Drain the bulgur wheat through a fine sieve and remove any excess water with paper kitchen towel. The bulgur wheat will swell to double its original size. Leave to dry thoroughly for about 10–20 minutes.

3 Place the bulgur wheat in a large bowl, add the lemon juice, the oil and a little salt and pepper. Allow to stand for 1–2 hours if possible, in order for the flavours to soak in to the bulgur wheat.

4 Add the parsley, mint, spring onions and green pepper and mix well. Chill until required. Serve at room temperature, garnished with tomatoes and black olives.

COOK'S TIP
Tabbouleh can be served with warm pitta bread or wrapped in lettuce leaves and eaten using your fingers. It also makes a filling side salad.

SPICED RICE

Rice is an important staple in Jewish cooking. It is served for both everyday meals and feasts. Spices, nuts and dried fruits are used here to make simple, boiled rice into a special dish, which can be eaten hot or cold.

INGREDIENTS
225g/8oz/1 cup basmati rice
30ml/2 tbsp oil
2.5cm/1in cinnamon stick
1.5ml/¼ tsp ground turmeric
1.5ml/¼ tsp tomato purée
15ml/1 tbsp raisins
salt and ground black pepper
25g/1oz toasted almonds, to serve

SERVES 4 – 6

COOK'S TIP
To remove the starch from rice, wash it thoroughly before and after boiling. For fried rice, boil the rice and pour cold water through it; leave to cool. Continue from Step 3, making sure the rice is quite hot before serving.

1 Using a sieve, rinse the rice in cold running water until the water runs clear. (See Cook's Tip above.)

2 Add the rice to a saucepan of boiling water. Add 5ml/1 tsp salt and boil for about 5–7 minutes or until the grains are tender. Drain and rinse through with a little boiling water.

3 To fry the rice, heat the oil in a large frying pan. Add the cinnamon stick and the turmeric and then the boiled rice. Stir well and heat thoroughly. Add the tomato purée and the raisins. Season with salt and pepper to taste.

4 Remove the cinnamon stick with a fork and serve, sprinkled with almonds.

AUBERGINES WITH GARLIC AND TOMATO GLAZE

Aubergines are usually fried, a method that makes them absorb large amounts of oil. Here they are roasted in the oven, which makes them less oily, and slightly crisp.

INGREDIENTS
2 aubergines, about 225g/8oz each
2 garlic cloves
45ml/3 tbsp tomato purée
90–120ml/6–8 tbsp olive oil
2.5ml/^{1}/$_2$ tsp sugar
salt and ground black pepper
flat leaf parsley, to garnish

SERVES 4

COOK'S TIP
If you like your aubergines oily, fry each slice in a shallow pan for about 5–10 minutes, on both sides. Top with the glaze and bake in the oven for 5 minutes before serving.

1 Slice the aubergines about 5mm/¼in thick and spread them out on kitchen paper. Sprinkle with salt and leave for about 30 minutes. The salt will remove any bitter taste from the aubergines.

2 Preheat the oven to 190ºC/375ºF/Gas 5. Crush the garlic cloves into a small bowl and stir in the tomato purée, 15ml/1 tbsp oil, sugar and the seasoning. Pour about 60ml/4 tbsp oil into a baking tin.

3 Rinse the aubergine slices in water, drain and dry them well. Arrange them over the oiled tin in a single layer. Spoon a little of the garlic tomato mixture over each one. Drizzle over the remaining oil and bake the slices for about 30 minutes.

4 Carefully lift them off with a palette knife and arrange them, slightly overlapping, in a circle on a flat dish. Garnish with chopped parsley.

POTATO SALADS

Most people adore potato salad made with a creamy dressing. These two versions are light and summery, and ideal for buffets. The first should be served warm – the second can be prepared a day ahead and served cold.

INGREDIENTS
900g/2lb new potatoes
5ml/1 tsp salt

DRESSING FOR WARM SALAD
30ml/2 tbsp hazelnut or walnut oil
60ml/4 tbsp sunflower oil
juice of 1 lemon
15 pistachio nuts
salt and ground black pepper
flat leaf parsley, to garnish

DRESSING FOR COLD SALAD
a bunch of parsley (about 90ml/6 tbsp)
2 large spring onions
75ml/5 tbsp olive oil
10ml/2 tsp white wine vinegar
1 garlic clove, crushed
salt and ground black pepper

SERVES 4

1 Scrub the new potatoes thoroughly. Place in a pan, cover with cold water and bring to the boil. Add the salt and cook for about 10–15 minutes until the potatoes are tender. Drain well and set aside.

2 To make the warm salad, mix together the hazelnut or walnut oil with the sunflower oil and lemon juice and season well with salt and pepper.

3 Remove the shells from the pistachio nuts and discard. Using the flat side of a knife, or a pestle and mortar, crush the nuts roughly and set aside.

4 When the potatoes have cooled slightly, pour over the dressing and sprinkle with the chopped nuts. Serve garnished with flat leaf parsley.

5 For the cold salad, cook the potatoes as described above, drain and leave to cool. Meanwhile chop the parsley and the spring onions finely and add to the potatoes.

6 Whisk together the oil, vinegar, garlic and seasoning and pour over the potatoes. Cover tightly and chill overnight in a refrigerator. Allow to come to room temperature before serving.

POTATO LATKES

L atkes, or pancakes, should be piping hot and are traditionally served with hot salt beef. Alternatively, serve as a snack with apple sauce and soured cream.

INGREDIENTS
2 medium potatoes
1 onion
1 large egg, beaten
30ml/2 tbsp medium-ground matzo meal
oil, for frying
salt and ground black pepper

SERVES 4

1 Grate the potatoes and the onion coarsely. Place in a large colander. Using the back of a large spoon, press the mixture down, squeezing out the starchy liquid.

2 Transfer the potato mixture to a large bowl. Beat the egg lightly in another bowl. Immediately pour the egg into the drained potato and onion mixture and stir well. Add the matzo meal, mixing thoroughly. Season well.

3 Pour some oil into a frying pan to a depth of about 1cm/½in. Heat the oil for a few minutes (test it by throwing a small piece of bread into the oil, which should sizzle). Take a spoonful of the *latke* mixture and lower carefully into the oil. Continue adding spoonfuls, not too close together, over the base of the pan.

4 Flatten the pancakes slightly with the back of a spoon and, after a few minutes when the *latkes* are golden brown on one side, carefully turn them over and continue frying until the other side is golden brown.

5 Remove from the frying pan with a slotted spoon or spatula. Drain the *latkes* on kitchen paper and serve immediately.

DATE BREAD

Dates have been used in cooking since biblical times. Dried fruits have a natural sweetness, so this loaf needs no added sugar.

INGREDIENTS
225g/8oz/1⅓ cups dried dates
2.5ml/½ tsp bicarbonate of soda
150ml/¼ pint/⅔ cup boiling water
1 egg
15g/½oz butter softened
150g/5oz/⅔ cup self-raising flour
lightly salted butter, to serve

MAKES 1 LOAF – 16 SLICES

1 Preheat the oven to 160°C/325°F/Gas 3. Chop the dates and place in a bowl with the bicarbonate of soda and boiling water. Leave the dates to soak for about 5 minutes.

2 Grease and line a 450g/1lb loaf tin with buttered greaseproof paper so that it comes to at least 2.5cm/1in above the tin.

3 Stir the egg, butter and flour into the date mixture and beat until smooth. The small pieces of date give the bread texture. Pour the mixture into the prepared tin.

4 Bake for about 1 hour in the centre of the oven. To test if the loaf is cooked, insert a strand of raw spaghetti or a thin skewer into its centre. The spaghetti or skewer should emerge without any signs of moisture if properly cooked. Remove from the oven when ready and leave to cool.

5 When the bread is cold, take it out of the tin and remove the paper. Serve sliced and buttered.

CHALLAH

laited *challah* loaves are traditionally served at Sabbath meals and festivals.

INGREDIENTS
450g/1lb/4 cups strong white flour
7.5ml/1½ tsp salt
10ml/2 tsp caster sugar (optional)
10ml/2 tsp quick-acting dried yeast
45ml/3 tbsp oil
250ml/8fl oz/1 cup warm water
2 eggs
poppy seeds, to decorate

MAKES 2 LOAVES

1 Sift together the flour, salt and sugar, if using, and sprinkle over the yeast. Mix the oil, half of the water and 1 egg together. The water must be warm; if too hot or too cold, the bread won't rise. Add the rest of the water to the flour and then the oil and egg mixture.

2 Mix together until a dough is formed, then knead until smooth and elastic, using a little extra flour if it seems sticky.

3 Put the dough in a greased bowl, cover with a clean dish towel and leave in a warm place for at least 2 hours.

4 Knock back the dough by kneading it and then divide it into two. Cut each piece into three and roll them into long sausage shapes. Using three strands for each loaf, plait the dough.

5 Tuck the ends of each plait underneath and leave the plaited loaves to rise on an oiled baking sheet for about 30 minutes.

6 Preheat the oven to 220°C/425°F/Gas 7. Brush the loaves with the remaining beaten egg and sprinkle with poppy seeds.

7 Bake for about 35–40 minutes. Leave to cool on a wire tray for 5–10 minutes. Serve with butter, hot or cold.

CINNAMON ROLLS

These spicy pastries are perfect for breakfast or tea, served fresh and spread with butter, if desired.

INGREDIENTS
FOR THE DOUGH
400g/14oz/1²/₃ cups strong white flour
2.5ml/¹/₂ tsp salt
30ml/2 tbsp sugar
5ml/1 tsp quick-acting dried yeast
45ml/3 tbsp oil
1 egg
120ml/4fl oz/¹/₂ cup warm milk
120ml/4fl oz/¹/₂ cup warm water

FOR THE FILLING
25g/1oz butter, softened
25g/1oz dark brown sugar
2.5–5ml/¹/₂–1 tsp ground cinnamon
15ml/1 tbsp raisins or sultanas

MAKES 24 SMALL ROLLS

1 Sift the flour, salt and sugar, and sprinkle over the yeast. Mix the oil, egg, milk and water and add to the flour. Mix to a dough, then knead thoroughly until smooth. Leave to rise until doubled in size and then knock it back again.

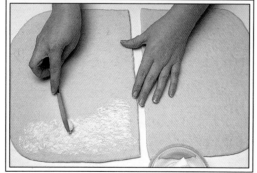

2 Roll out the dough into a large rectangle and cut in half vertically. Spread butter over each half, reserving 15ml/1 tbsp for brushing. Mix the sugar and cinnamon and sprinkle over the top. Dot with the raisins.

3 Roll each piece into a long Swiss roll shape, to enclose the filling. Cut into 2.5cm/1in slices, arrange flat on a greased baking sheet and brush with the remaining butter. Leave to prove again for about 30 minutes.

4 Preheat the oven to 200ºC/400ºF/Gas 6 and bake the cinnamon rolls for about 20 minutes. Leave to cool on a wire rack. Serve fresh with extra butter, if preferred.

NOODLE PUDDING

Noodle Pudding is a rich and comforting dessert. This dish is never served after a meat course as it contains cheese and cream.

INGREDIENTS
175g/6oz wide egg noodles
225g/8oz cottage cheese
115g/4oz cream cheese
75g/3oz/¹/₃ cup caster sugar
2 eggs
120ml/4fl oz/¹/₂ cup soured cream
25g/1oz/¹/₄ cup raisins
5ml/1 tsp vanilla essence
pinch of ground cinnamon
pinch of grated nutmeg
2.5ml/¹/₂ tsp grated lemon rind
50g/2oz butter
25g/1oz/¹/₄ cup almonds, chopped
25g/1oz/¹/₄ cup fine dried white breadcrumbs
icing sugar for dusting
sprig of mint, to serve (optional)

SERVES 4 – 6

1 Preheat the oven to 180ºC/350ºF/Gas 4. Grease a shallow baking dish. Cook the noodles in a large saucepan of boiling water until just tender. Drain well.

2 Beat the cottage cheese, cream cheese and sugar together in a bowl. Add the eggs, one at a time, and stir in the soured cream. Stir in the raisins, vanilla essence, cinnamon, nutmeg and lemon rind.

3 Fold the noodles into the cheese mixture. Spoon into the prepared baking dish and level the surface.

4 Melt the butter in a frying pan. Add the almonds and fry for about 1 minute. Remove from the heat.

5 Stir in the breadcrumbs, mixing well. Sprinkle the mixture over the pudding. Bake for 30–40 minutes or until the mixture is set. Serve hot, dusted with a little icing sugar and a sprig of mint, if desired.

FRUIT TREE PIE

 A pie for Tu B'Shvat, a celebration at the end of winter, when the almond trees blossom in Israel.

INGREDIENTS
FOR THE PASTRY
150g/5oz/²/₃ cup kosher margarine
225g/8oz/2 cups plain flour
1 egg, separated
60ml/4 tbsp cold water

FOR THE FILLING
450g/1lb cooking apples, or fresh apricots or plums, stoned
60–120ml/4–8 tbsp sugar

SERVES 4 – 6

1 To make the pastry, chill the margarine and then rub into the flour until it looks like breadcrumbs. Add the egg yolk and water, mix and form the dough into a ball. Cover and chill the dough for 30 minutes.

2 Preheat the oven to 200°C/400°F/Gas 6. Peel and core the apples or stone the apricots or plums, if using. On a piece of paper, draw and cut out a tree shape about 30cm/12in high.

3 Roll out the pastry to approximately 1cm/½in thick and put the tree outline on top. Cut round the tree and then repeat, cutting a second tree about 1cm/½in larger. Using a spatula or palette knife, carefully lift the tree shapes off the pastry board on to a baking tray.

4 Take the smaller tree shape and cover with thinly sliced apples, or the stoned fruit. Sprinkle over the sugar to taste, reserving 15ml/1 tbsp for the top.

5 Cover the pie with the larger tree outline, firmly pressing it down at the edges. Whisk the egg white lightly and brush it all over the pie. Roll out the pastry trimmings and cut out some apple or plum shapes. Press these on to the tree and brush again with egg white. Sprinkle over the remaining sugar and bake for about 30–35 minutes.

6 Remove the baking sheet from the oven. Slide a palette knife carefully underneath the pie and when it has cooled, transfer it to a large platter.

PEACH KUCHEN

The joy of this cake is its all-in-one simplicity. It can be served hot and moist, straight from the oven, or cut into squares when cold.

INGREDIENTS
350g/12oz/3 cups self-raising flour
225g/8oz/1 cup caster sugar
175g/6oz/³/₄ cup unsalted butter, softened
2 eggs
120ml/4fl oz/¹/₂ cup milk
6 large peeled peaches, sliced or
450g/1lb plums or cherries, stoned
115g/4oz/¹/₂ cup soft brown sugar
2.5ml/¹/₂ tsp ground cinnamon
soured cream, to serve (optional)

SERVES 8

1 Preheat the oven to 190°C/375°F/Gas 5. Grease and line a 20 x 25 x 2.5cm/ 8 x 10 x 1in cake tin.

2 Put the flour, caster sugar, butter, eggs and milk into a large bowl and beat for a few minutes until you have a smooth batter. Spoon it into the prepared cake tin.

3 Skin and stone the ripe peaches, plums or cherries (see Cook's Tip) and slice into small, even-sized chunks. Arrange the fruit over the cake mixture.

4 Mix together the brown sugar and cinnamon and sprinkle over the fruit.

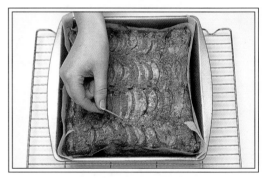

5 Bake for about 40 minutes, testing when it is cooked by inserting a cocktail stick in the centre, which should emerge clean.

6 Serve the cake warm or cool with the soured cream, if using.

COOK'S TIP
To skin peaches, or other soft fruit, plunge into boiling water for 20 seconds.

COCONUT PYRAMIDS

Coconut is a traditional Passover ingredient for cakes, biscuits and pastries. They are sold piled high on Israeli street market stalls.

INGREDIENTS
225g/8oz/1 cup unsweetened
desiccated coconut
115g/4oz/¹/₂ cup caster sugar
2 egg whites
oil, for greasing

MAKES 15

1 Preheat the oven to 190°C/375°F/Gas 5. Grease a large baking sheet with a little of the oil.

2 Mix together the desiccated coconut and the sugar. Lightly whisk the egg whites. Fold enough egg white into the coconut to make a fairly firm mixture. You may not need all the egg whites.

3 Form the mixture into pyramid shapes by taking a teaspoonful and first rolling it into a ball. Flatten the base and press the top into a point. Arrange the pyramids on a greased baking sheet, leaving a space between them.

4 Bake for 12–15 minutes on a low shelf. The tips should begin to turn golden and the pyramids should be just firm, but still soft inside.

5 Slide a palette knife under the pyramids to loosen them, and leave to cool before removing from the baking sheet.

CINNAMON BALLS

Ground almonds or hazelnuts form the basis of most Passover cakes and biscuits. These balls should be soft inside, with a very strong cinnamon flavour. They harden with keeping, so it is a good idea to freeze some and defrost them only when required.

INGREDIENTS
175g/6oz/1½ cups ground almonds
75g/3oz/⅓ cup caster sugar
15ml/1 tbsp ground cinnamon
2 egg whites
oil for greasing
icing sugar, for dredging

MAKES 15

COOK'S TIP
Cinnamon Balls should be stored in an airtight container to keep fresh. If freezing, do so as soon as they are cool. They will keep for up to six weeks in the freezer.

1 Preheat the oven to 180ºC/350ºF/Gas 4. Grease a large baking sheet with oil.

2 Mix together the almonds, sugar and cinnamon. In a separate bowl, whisk the egg whites until they begin to stiffen and then fold enough into the almond mixture to make a firm consistency.

3 Wet your hands with cold water and roll small spoonfuls of the mixture into balls. Place these at intervals on the baking sheet.

4 Bake for 15 minutes in the centre of the oven. They should be slightly soft inside – too much cooking will make them tough.

5 Slide a palette knife under the balls to release them from the baking sheet and leave to cool.

6 Sift a few tablespoons of icing sugar on to a plate. When the cinnamon balls are cold slide them onto the plate. Shake gently to completely cover the balls in sugar. Serve with black coffee or afternoon tea.

INDEX